D0019226

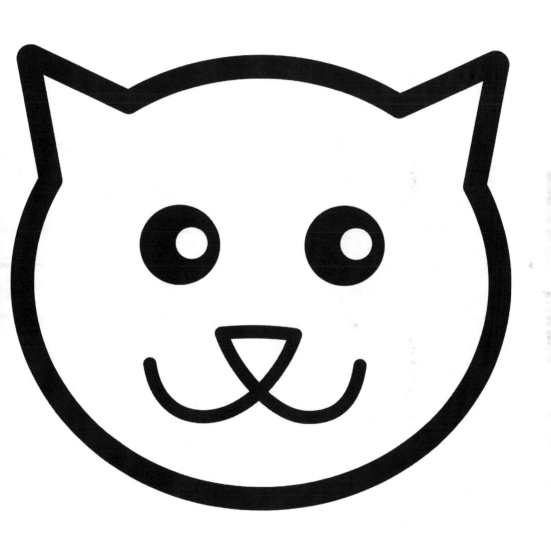

From birth your baby is naturally drawn to bold shapes and they absolutely love faces – especially yours!

Cuddle up nice and close and show your baby the patterns, shapes and faces - see how they react - which is their favorite?

Listen out for a gurgle and look for changes in your baby's facial expression - that's your baby trying to talk to you about what they see!

Your baby may lose interest - this is completely normal as babies can tire easily. Little and often is best.

Lots of noise in the background can be distracting - turn off the TV and put away your mobile phone. Give your full undivided attention.

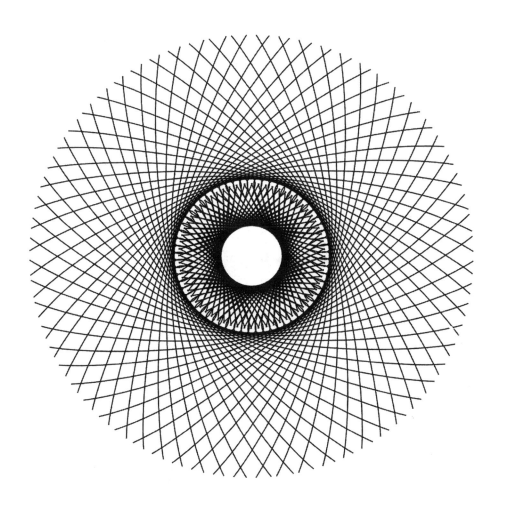

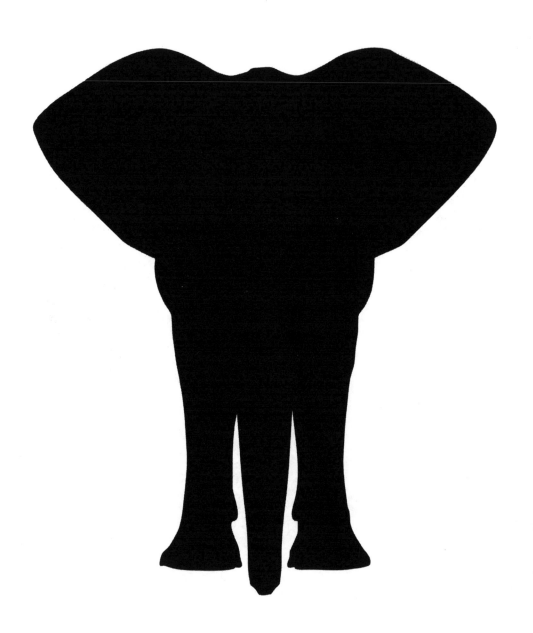